Air Histories

Also by Christopher Meredith

Poems
This
Snaring Heaven
The Meaning of Flight
Black Mountains: poems & images
from the Bog~Mawnog Project

Novels
Shifts
Griffri
Sidereal Time
The Book of Idiots

For children
Nadolig bob Dydd
Christmas Every Day

As editor
Moment of Earth
Five Essays on Translation (with Katja Krebs)

Translation
Melog a novel by Mihangel Morgan

Air Histories
Christopher Meredith

SEREN

Seren is the book imprint of
Poetry Wales Press Ltd.
57 Nolton Street, Bridgend, Wales, CF31 3AE
www.serenbooks.com
Facebook: facebook.com/SerenBooks
Twitter: @SerenBooks

ISBN: 978-1-78172-074-5
ISBN e-book: 978-1-78172-076-9

A CIP record for this title is available from the British Library.

The publisher acknowledges the financial assistance of the Welsh Books Council.

Cover photograph: 'Daedalus with a paramotor' © V. Meredith.

Printed in Bembo by Berforts Group, Stevenage.

Author's Website: http://christophermeredith.webs.com/

Contents

Arrowhead

fire
unlock
ed the mou
ntain and rain
and wind brush
ed earth by to strip
to air what's reified
in stone, green double
wavelets in a piece of sea
jade flatfish swimming time
a hardening of fallen sky that
should whisper *death* or *meat* but
somehow can't becoming something
never meant in all the patient knapping
to perfected brittle symmetry strange midair
fingerprint stone cursor pointing to this hour
flint promise of our later fire that never
flew or sang till
now

Borderland

Ffin is the Welsh for border. It occurs inside diffiniad which means definition, and in Capel y Ffin, a place in the Black Mountains.

You'll find a *ffin* inside each definition.
We see what is when we see what it's not:
edges are where meanings happen.

On the black whaleback of this mountain
earth curves away so sky can start
to show a *ffin's* a kind of definition

where skylarks climb across earth's turn
to air and pulsing muscle turns to an art-
ful song the edge that lets a meaning happen.

Live rock can yield to mortared stone,
a city to a castle, then a shepherd's hut,
where *ffin's* contained inside a definition,

where the lithic turns into the human.
Here's where things fall together, not apart
at edges that let meanings happen.

And self here blurs into annihilation.
Larkfall, earthfall, skyfall, manfall each create
the *ffin* that is the place of definition
the edges where we see our meanings happen.

Trees on Castell Dinas

Stripped to their themes
the winter trees
are the sum of their seasons

bombbursts of filaments
in pulsing harmonics
enact their contentions in air

work into eyesight
with ogive writhing
invisible veins of the wind

solidify rhythms
into the pathways
of hunger for light

What earth thought

When wind blows to kill rain, earth
thinks warmer under sun and breathes
smoke. Grass squeezes out of stone,
walks under tree and over mountain.
Man walks with animals under moon.
Dog drinks lake. Child sucks woman.

Child sleeps with smell of milk and woman
who sings to call the seed from earth.
Man sings to beasts. Dog sings to moon.
They turn their hunger into breath.
They walk the belly of the mountain.
They hit the yellow fire from stone.

And what swells in grass, with stone
and stone they kill. The woman
burns seed under mountain.
They laugh it out from blackened earth.
They turn their hunger out of breath.
They sleep beneath the bitten moon.

The river's warm with yellow moon
swimming above the river stones.
They sing the songs of warmth, and breathe
the song of meat and fruits. The woman
knows that ice will bite the earth
and grass sleep again on mountain.

Black cloud will kill white, and mountain
float in lakes of rain. The moon
will die, and snow will say to earth:
whiten now and sleep. Push stones
out of your skin. And singing, the woman
will turn her hunger into breath

and a child may turn her breath
to not breath and the mountain
eat her and the singing woman
turn fear to white breath, but the moon
will stand in sky a dead stone
above hard lake and sleeping earth.

If woman's blood can sing to moon,
when wind's breath kills the rain on mountain
grass may walk again through stone and earth.

The record keepers

One thousand one hundred and thirty was the age of
Christ when there were four years in succession without
there being any history...
 – Brut y Tywysogyon/Chronicle of the Princes

That day, Brother Cynan in his magpie habit
stepped from the Scriptorium door.
Daniel and Owain paced by the pond
measured steps kicking at their gowns
and talked unheard.
Cynan threw crumbs to the sparrows,
rubbed his whiskery tonsure,
felt food easing through him, sighed
and looked back to the silent page.
    Rain fell then didn't.
The wheel of the sky
did its diurnal turn, its equinoctial tilt.
He slept and woke,
stared back at Taurus's red eye.
The masses passed.
    Was God asleep
or was this an awakening?
    One day in a ripening barley field
Cynan watched the quietness of butterflies,
white and many mazing and dipping
to blooms among the stalks.
They wrote the history of air.

★

Consider. The edited highlight could also be
the bit where the wicketkeeper yawns
rubbing an eyelash from his face.
Or think of Watts's minotaur –
he *could* be waiting on those battlements
for the freight of virgins, but maybe not,
that crushed bird no symbol, just a slip.
Perhaps there's no more narrative
than watching sky.

★

Then, at the bottom of a sea
like a hell on a church wall
hagfish fattened on a rotting monster
blind jaws working.
Fished up, they oozed and rotted in the sun.
And then a monster battened on bad meat
and found it good, till
suddenly he stopped.
Some inconsequential picture
stayed on his dying retinas –
a cobweb in a corner, say,
as his brain shut down.
A courtier will have hesitated,
checked for breath, flicked at last
a finger at the still eye
(in the royal jelly the unseen image
of the cobweb shivers)
and hurried out.
So in the rigor mortis of a king
Process stiffened to event and story woke
and plot and consequence began again.

★

Brother Cynan in his magpie habit
took his knife and opened the Scriptorium door.
Somewhere in him till he died would be
an unheard talk, some sparrows on a path
small scriptless books that eddied in still air.
    He said, *The thing about the ineffable is* –
and shrugged and pared the quill,
split the nib, and reached for ink.

Y grib

Enw'r Saeson ar y grib yw *cefn y ddraig*.
Addas i'r rhai sydd angen anghenfilod saff
mewn chwedlau dôf.
Ynom mae'r gwir anghenfil.
Edrychwch − ôl yr anadl llosg,
y cafnau hir lle bu'r crafangau.

Na. Llinell alaw ydyw
                    o graig
                     a phridd
              ffiwg o rythmau
                        yn esgyn
                         a disgyn
                              ac esgyn
                            curiad ymdrech
            a saib   ac ymdrech
                      a saib
                    cymalau esgyrnog
                              y cefn
                               yn codi
                          mewn llif
                            nodiadau sy'n
                            newid eu lliw
                            dan lusgo'r
                        cymylau dros haul
                                esgyn i'r ffin
                          ar yr uwchdir hwnnw
                              sy'n brathu'r
                                      awyr
                               a chyrraedd
                               y distawrwydd
                                 ar ddiwedd
                                        y gân

Ridge

In English it's *the dragon's back*, a name
for those who like their monsters
safely mythic, tame.
The real monster's here.
See where our burning breath has passed,
The places that the talons tear.

No. It's a line
      of music
    made in stone
         and earth
      repeated rising figure of
                  effort,
            rest
      and rest   and effort
           of vertebra like
    an arpeggio
        taking
           colour
   from those clouds that blow
              across the sun
        falling
       and swelling
      to where that edge
             of upland
              bites
                the sky
              goes home
             resolves at last
           to almost-silence in
                white noise of
                  living air

At Colonus

Variations on a line from Dorothy Edwards

```
  N       a
      m                   e
      m  y     t      est.
         A       t      r          y
                          st,
         a       t
o                        r
  n              n      est
         a               re
      m  y
      ma        t        t       e
                         r. St
              o          r
      m                  re
              n  t        s
   e      a               s
      may                         t
                         r        y
      ma                  s         t
              o          r
o         a              r  s
              o          r
      ma                  st      e
                         r  s
                                  yet
            no            st
o                        r
      m                   s        t
                         r        y
      m                  e.
         A                s       y
   e      a              r  s
                          s        e
         a               r
      m  y                e        ye
```

```
                    no        r
            ay                s
            may
              a     n
  n                 o                   y
            m                 e.
            M y       t       e
              a               r  s
              a               re
                                st
  on                          es.
  One               not       e's
                    no
            m       ot                  et
  one       ma      n
    n               o
              a               r
            m   y,                      yet
              a       t       re        e
            may               r
  o                 ot
  on                          st
  one.      M       ot       es
              a               re    ye
              a                st,
                      t       e         e
            m                 s
  o         ma                r  s
  o                           r
            m       o
  on                          s
            may               r
  o           a               r.
```

17

```
            A              e
o              n           s
         a              r           e
      m        o
      m                 e
               n t      s,
                        st
         a              r s
         a              r           e
         a        t
o        m              s.
                        S           et
      m                 e
on.              T      est
      m                 e           yet.
                        St
         ay    n                    e
         a              r,
O     m  y     o
  ne                    st
         a              r,
      m  y              st
               o        r
         y,    t      est
      m                             y
         a        t
one   m                 e
               n  t.
               No       rest.
One   may     not      rest.
One   may     not      rest      yet.
```

18

The churches

We live in low places
or on mountaintops.
Don't expect us to aspire.
Skyward fingers
are for foreigners.
If we risk a tower
it squats hard
and burrows toes in shale,
glances up the better to know
its downhereness.

   No. Down's where to knuckle,
clench mud
and honour stone
with our stoniness.
We fasten to hinterlands
or cling to edges
in the turn of light round cloud
where hill slithers into cliff
where mountain arches into air
where snouts of land
push into sea
that turns to light
and light that liquefies.

   But at the base all's earth.
It's said what's wired to rock
can draw down thunderbolts.
There are rumours of gods.
Don't trust them.
Expect no communing.
We draw you from people
to bare ledges
to woodclogged hollows
where old lonely life
endures under thorn or carapace,
to far places where
on the good days
pure water seeps
from mud.

The guitar maker Antonio de Torres in old age described by the priest Juan Martínez Sirvent

Dear Friend,
To answer your delightful letter,
these words.

Yes, I knew your ancestor.
He was a calm man of grave mind.
His hand shook a little;
his eye was steady as his measured voice.
When he revealed to us with his cítara,
his favourite instrument,
which he had also made himself,
his compositions,
he became a poet
of intimate gatherings.

And there were times
and many
when he asked my help to glue
the ribs and soundboards
and the backs and inlays and rosettes.
He'd shut and lock the workshop door.
It seemed his due to treat his young priest
as apprentice.

★

On a saint's day once
to enhance solemnity I gathered
don Emilio Jiménez to celebrate the mass
don Serafín Abad as organist
my cousin don Miguel Sirvent to read the collect
and, great fortune, Father Garzón,
then instructing priests in Almería –
yes, and Master Torres too
to lunch in honour among holy men.

After the meal: 'Don Antonio,'
great Garzón said, 'death is long
and always sooner than we want.
You must let the secret of your art
into the world.'
The old man smiled and looked from him to me.
'Juanito has been witness to this secret
many times.'
He gestured me to speak.

I was a young man then.
I thought of the locked door, the frets and clamps,
the workshop's silence, calm and tense,
the heaped old furniture he'd work
into the boxes and the necks
the air of rosewood coming off the blade,
of his hands, trembling among the bars and straps,
my own hand steady as his voice, his eye –
but blind, just doing as he said.

What could I do but shrug
and turn away?
Above the tablecloth the Master Torres
raised a hand that shook a little even then
and looked into the tremulous gap
between the fingertips and thumb.
A pinch of air
was all he had.

★

That was fifty years ago and now
his work is his witness.
If witness was my work
perhaps I had to come terms with mysteries
or perhaps I failed.

Friend, for this history I ask
one favour:
send me the news of Almería.
Though I am old I hunger still
to know the way of things.

The ones with the white hats

After it was over
it started.
We stopped fighting and got in ships.
We stopped off at islands
to bury rotting people.

In the city-state where they bayoneted
patients in their beds
we restored order.
We shot the looters in the streets.
We rounded their men up.
In the Chinese camp where they'd starved us
we put them
and fed them well.
Nights when they crossed the yard to the shithouse
we shot them and dragged them to the fence.
They were always trying to escape like that.

We took them back to their home
in the holds of coal ships,
whatever we could get.
On deck we got sick as dogs.
We didn't check too hard below.
We stopped at Nagasaki for a look.
The double-tap that clinched it.

At some northern island
don't know what it's called
we put in, ran them not quite naked
down the gangplank to the quay.
It was snowing.
We made them stand
and heaped what kit they had
and burned it.
Smoke was the only smell.
Flames were the only colour.

Birth myth

These signs have marked me extraordinary

'At my nativity
The front of heaven was full of fiery shapes.'
Well, snow. Full of snow.
But don't we hunger for the birth myth,
to be like Madam Patti littered
on a stage midway through the opera
our diva mother going back on for the aria
the birthmess trailing in her skirts
and hitting the next note in the middle
or to emerge from an improbable bodypart
of some blurry cosmic protogod
quite possibly of the wrong sex
in a tale magnificently heedless
of the needs of the chronotope
or to rise from the profoundest cave
in a burning plain on a mountaintop
and father godlets of our own
or to be sired by Jupiter
while some earthly husband sleeps
and be halfbrother to mere fleshliness
and then to strangle boa constrictors
while lying in our cot
or (dare I?) to gurgle in a starry crib
at three grandees with dusty boots
abasing themselves, presenting their gifts
and baldspots?

But in my case it was snow.
I know because my parents told me so.
Infant amnesia pins the rap
on what you half remember half make up
of what your parents half remembered
half made up. In that sense, yes, it's myth
though I've sort of checked. There's a photo

from that winter, Tŷ Trist Pit, silhouettes
just up from the face,
hunched in daicaps crossing a gantry,
a journey of coalfilled drams snowplastered,
the white ridged deep on bashed black girderwork,
heaped props, the roofs of sheds, and beyond,
the valley doing postwar bleak,
blurring to a nowhere without gods.

Yes, there was snow.
It lay deep in Market Street
– the name's an *Ithaca, Persepolis* –
from the Town Clock up the hill
to Saron Chapel where Ieuan Gwynedd
had preached against Blue Books,
and she, my mother, twenty-nine
and fragile from the deaths of babies
carried me that first time
in the open air.
Think of the snowdust fizzing in her throat
and then the sudden alp on the pavement
that almost killed us both.
So the earth did shake when I was born,
a little. There must have been that hissing slither
and the flumping crunch,
the sound of something almost happening
senselessly. This marks me ordinary.
A woman with a baby in a whitened street
that closes in behind her
walking towards eternity from the clock
uphill, in the cold.

The slurry pond

My heartland was a place of edges
                    though I scarcely knew it.
Limestone pavement turned to sand,
                    coal surfacing, becoming air
edge of a shadow on a lung
                    where whole replaces hurt.
And time, too, kept a border
                    broken backed across a war.

A ruined city lay around *us*
                    in our infancy
– the pumping station, railless sidings,
                    workings of an age
we didn't realise was not quite dead.
                    Such rubbish we
played among. We saw no edge
                    between the natural and made.

Quarries and cliffs, moor and shaletip
                    all were the garden of our
innocence. Still we knew
                    that other edge that drew us
in the shocked gougings of the opencast,
                    its bright lochs poison,
its crumbling lips, in old shafts that bid
                    us fall. And yes, in the sour
black slurry pumped from flooded pits.
                    Its edge was hardened pus
we'd walk, each step yielding softer till
                    its mud heart sucked you down.

Daniel's piano

Daniel's piano stands next to the table.
Its keyboard is open. Its smile is yellow.

Daily Simon arranges the table –
some vases, some flowers. The tureen steams.

Outside in the larches the bee-eaters settle.
The Haifa road's quiet. The cooling coast's hazy.

The guests push away plates and sit back at sunset.
They're full. All's calm. There's civilised talk.

Simon stands in the doorway.
He's content. He says nothing.

The bust of young Daniel also
says nothing. It smiles at the guests.

In his painting, aged ten,
he sits at the keyboard. He smiles at the future.

The long lid is shut. The boxed harp says nothing.
So sad, they all say. Long past, but so sad.

Daniel's house stands
on a village they emptied.

Nobody talks of the village's going.
Its old name is silenced.

Simon is a good man. His manner is gentle.
The guests discuss poetry. Nobody plays.

Guitar

The fringe of the sunshade changes
chords across the sky. I'm sorry

I didn't bring you here. You'd love
the hot dry air, cicadas

flirting with the quietness.
Darling, I miss you. I miss

your mellow cypress
your poise in silence

and how you answer my speaking
sometimes, always underplaying

my blah with harmonies
to make our scratch duet,

such unwitting consonance
such subtle stichomythia,

and I miss the glide of your mahogany
neck under the ball of my thumb

your elusive teasing when
we're easing into tune

the nuanced shifting of your moods
with moistened air and changing heat

how the harmonic struck on A
lives in you an age, gathers

a choir of others and swells and falls
walking your grounds

and your patience with my idiotic songs –
Fats Waller gone scrawny

my botched scraps of nearly Dowland –
the way that *you* play *me*

deep, opened rosewood
thrumming my ribs like a dulcimer

and, when we forget that we are two
just once in an unlikely while,

how close we get to something right
that's made of air and time

and understands its own brief thrill
between two silences.

Not quite Apollo

They took off for
the valley of the moon
but the signs ran out.

It must be either right or left, he said.
The road was windy.
They were uphill narrow ways.
The hire car was strange.
They drive in the middle, she said.
There'll be nothing there, he said.

And they sat outside a café
too scared to ask for milk for the tea.

The sun gave up and shrugged and turned to leave
and on a far ridge late rays caught
how huge and curious rocks were hunched
above some secret place.
The moon people were hitching up their shawls,
sniggering.

Think of this

Think of this:
two fish that hang
under the hammered
amber
of the stream

They coil at ease
brushing as they pass
knowing with each eddy
the presence of other
the soft oiled metal of their slipknot
tying and untying
mouthing agelong quietness

They need no dream
or wish for some
refracted paradise above
– they fall
forever as they turn
into the space where each just was
and flee and gleam
and fleeing almost meet

Think, to be them
have such repose in restlessness
two fish adrift and fixed
in endless revolution
of their almost
kiss

The strange music

The history says
two Spanish sisters of great quality,
Vitoria and Mercedes,
travelled from their exquisite wood
where the small birds joined in song

to Paris and to England
to discourse with the luthiers great,
René Francois Lacote
who studied much the chemistry of varnishes
and Signor Lovis Panormo
then resident in London Tower.

'Ladies, let us look upon the mast!'
cried M. Lacote. 'The fibre nerve!
The central nerve of cedar!
It makes visible the dark dense grain.
It contributes to the mast rigidity!'

'Oh, allow,' the sisters said,
'a better answer in vibration.
Extend the surface of the sound
To brighten the interiors.'

Signor Panormo, palps at the fingerboard,
felt rosewood open to his touch
and shuddered.

Listener, cast a glance at the mouth,
the gorgeous mouth whose fir
is of first quality.
Adorning it is the rosette
that is made not only with much love
but patience also.

And the signor and the monsieur and the sisters
were hallucinated by the song of the mouth.

★

Deep in a sunless grove
under a jacaranda tree
sat Palisander the Philosopher,
dedicated in body and soul,
polishing thought to the minimum detail.

The ideal wood
is difficult to cut
and hard to carve.
One reaches not
such perfection,
not in the sunless grove
nor all the forests
that will ever be.
but I will strive
in the dark wood
for the good orchestra.
For the song is worth
the ache in the hands
the agony, the work.

And in darkness and alone
in silence
he sat and sat and sat.

★

Far out
   in the longitudinal pitching of the sea
      on board the *Griffbrett*'s polished deck,
         the fisherman, old Palometas of Nacar,
            dismissed the mechanics in their
               gilded buttons

and listened to the deep,
      how she conserved the classic measures
         the searching harmony

and he cried out: 'That mountain body!
                That sonorous curve
            that hoops the radius of the earth
                to wake all griefs –
                that sound!
That sound is warm and sweet,
                and very burdensome.'

                                And he wept
                for the voices of drowned friends.
                    Old Keller, Palosanto, Palorosa
long dead, encoralled in the turbid banks
under his tarstained heels.

★

So the sisters woke among the stony towers.
The luthiers straightened their cravats,
did not admit to the trembling nerve in man,
were, rather, calm and circumspect.

'Non-single is aesthetic,' Vitoria said.
'These pins work firm and smooth,
but…'
– she looked to the woodland's edge –
'…towers and their concepts
hold us not.'

★

Much is written of origins.
There are the stone forests
and there is the ideal wood
and the dark wood
and the vein of the cedar that runs
like a sea in the other sense.

And then there is that exquisite wood
the sisters came home to
whose song was warmly deep and very sweet.
We celebrate it now in the classic mass.

Seeing the birds

Suddenly
he forgot the kettle.
Through the kitchen window
he could see the birds.

Though they hopped about
they were big as dogs,
fat dogs hopping in his garden.
The feathering on them
plates of black and brown
was sharp as the pattern on the kitchen tiles.
The crumbs they pecked at,
they were granite blocks.

The clacky beaks. The eyes.
They could tear the innards out of stone.
They could break down all the doors.
They could smash up all the clocks.
They could hop the world to smithereens.

Three years retired
and suddenly he saw the birds.

Look! Look! The eagles!
The eagles on the lawn!

Stori'r mynydd

Roedd gan y Groegiaid gynt
ddaear arall
'r ochr draw i'r haul –

mae rhai storïau'n byw
tu hwnt i ffin heb groesfan

ar blanedau anweledig
mewn gwledydd y tu draw
i ymyl map

neu mewn mannau cudd
agosach –
mae dreigiau
yn seler coll y castell
anghenfil dan y llyn
hanes dan glo
ym môn coed

ac yn agosach,
dan styllod stafell wely
yn y bwlch tu ôl
i'r cwpwrdd dillad
mewn onglau yn y drych
tu hwnt i dy lygaid di.

Ac ym meindwr tynn
y mynydd
lle rwyt ti'n sefyll nawr.

Dyma nenlofft gysglyd
ddieithr-gyfarwydd
dy blentyndod.

Pan gerddi di
lan fan 'na yng ngwynt y grib
cwyd lechen wen.
Edrycha lawr.
Ai gartre wyt ti?

Under the mountain

Some stories live
in places we can't go
on the planets no one's photographed
in countries off the edges of the maps

or in the closer hiddens
– that mother of monsters
under a lake
stories locked in the trunks
of trees –

and closer still
under the floorboards
in the space behind the wardrobe
in the angles in the mirror
you can never see.

And then there's the closed steeple
of this mountain
where you stand now
where the musician led the children
where kings lie asleep.
This is the dreaming attic of the house
familiar and strange
where you grew up.

When you walk up there
on the windcombed ridge
prise loose a whitened slate.
Look down.
See if you are home.

Alchemical

The hot water sweet from boiling spuds
drained in with the juices of the lamb

forgotten how
to check
the dates
on tins

and then the fluttering of the tablespoon
snowing flour to whiten and thicken

or how
to tune
the radio

and then the turning of the spoon
rattling the tin ribs of the casserole

even how
to make
welsh cakes

and then the crusted secret phial
the intense poured black thread

how to
wrap a
grandchild in
a shawl

lacing the vortex with absence
till a flower opens
the colour
yes
the colour of Sharp's toffee

She still works
the kitchen's casual miracle
three thousand Sundays
revolving under her hand

We must be the witnesses
She stirs and stirs and scarcely looks

Peth doeth

Peth doeth oedd dod
meddai'r doctor.

Crymais ysgwydd noeth.
Tynnodd allan dâp mesur.
Teimlo'r tafod dur
ar fy nghefn.
ymdrech i beidio â throi ac edrych.
gwrando ar
dri churiad o ddistawrwydd.

Dim byd i boeni amdano
eto.

Blaen meddal ei fys llaith
yn ysgafn dynnu ar draws
y cnawd tywyll, rhychog.
Cadwn lygad arno.
Ac yna, cynnig eli
i feddalu amser.

★

Hanner pryderon
oes ansicr yw'r rhain.
Y corff yn troi'n
frithdir fel hen gyfrol,
ffurfiau llosg yn lledaenu
yn wyddor ddi-synnwyr,
a'r ddalen yn troi
i'r un sepia â'r llythrennau.
Ffiniau'n diflannu.

Pridd ydwyf,
fy nghorff ar fainc meddyg
yn grib mynydd
a gwenwyn yn anadlu
o'r rhwyg du.

You were right to come

You were right to come
the doctor said.

I hunched a naked shoulder. He
uncoiled a metal tape –
the sort you'd use for DIY.
I felt its steel tag dig
into my back,
tried hard not to twist and look,
and I listened to his three beats' silence.

No need to worry
yet.

The palp of his finger, lightly,
tugged across the roughening browned flesh.
We'll keep an eye.
And then, the offer of emollient.

★

These are the not-quite-worries
of an uncertain age.
The body mottles
like a foxed old book.
The scorched shapes uncurl their serifs
that are the opposite of alphabets
and the page begins its turn
to the sepia of the text.
Definitions blur.

I am becoming earth
the ridge of me this mountain
its lesions breathing poison into air.

Twobeat deathsong

takemy	mother
fromher	window
she'sno	goodat
watching	mountains
takeher	tothe
running	waters
lether	hearthe
falling	fountains
Takemy	father
fromhis	garden
he'sno	goodat
scentsof	flowers
takehim	tothe
quiet	dayroom
lethim	tastethe
failing	hours
Takethem	fromme
tothe	river
letthem	touchthe
running	waters
takethem	fromme
tothe	dayroom
letthem	knowthe
falling	hours

Dream

We were walking
some interminable modern bridge
between a city and a city
– dreams permit themselves crass symbols –
and he was as he had been
fifteen, twenty years before,
wearing a familiar coat,
troubled in breathing,
tolerating the false teeth
but healthy, chatting.
The volume's low.
Lips move but I'm not quite catching
what we say. You know
the sort of thing.

And then, halfway of course,
he stopped and turned
and offered me his hand.
We had an absurd handshake
that we never had,
and he smiled, *smiled,*
an ordinary, half-facetious smile
as if this all was some light thing
some pale etiquette
to do with knowing when.

And someone turned the dial a touch
and two words came.
– *Well, goodbye.*
And he laughed.
We hung in air.
Below us was a river or the sea.

Life and death's as trite as that.
An unheard conversation
a clip of film
that doesn't say
which one is turning back
which going on.

Dim byd

Mae diwedd byd ymhob angau.
Mae diwedd syniadau
Ym mhylu'r ymennydd,
yn niwedd y niwronau,
mae tranc côf, tranc crebwyll
diwedd ystyr, diwedd iaith.
Mae gwreiddyn pob haniaeth
mewn pridd.

Ac ystyriwch sut mae llosgi crib
a rhwygo mynydd
yn agor drws ar ebargofiant.
yn rhychau du'r glaw
fe olchwn fyd i'r môr.
ym mlawd du'r hafau hesb
fe daflwn fyd i'r gwynt.
Craig noeth fydd gorsedd gwallgofrwydd,
a neb ar ôl i gyfri'r geiriau coll
heb ddim byd i dyfu ynddo –

grug y mêl
plu'r gweunydd
llysiau duon bach
corn carw'r mynydd
sidan y waun.

Nothing

Every death is a world's end.
In the synaptic powercut,
in the fading of a brain
is end of memory
end of synthesis
death of meaning
severing of tongues.
Each abstraction has its root in earth.

And think, how burning a ridge
gashing wide a mountaintop
opens the lid on nothingness.
In the black rutting of the rain
you wash a world into the sea
in blackened summer's dust
you toss a world into a hurricane.
Bared rock becomes the throne of senselessness
and no one will sit there to take a stock
of all the words
that have no earth to grow in –

ling
hare's tail cotton grass
whinberry
honey heather
meadow silk.

Bro Neb: yr arweinlyfr

Mae gan faner genedlaethol Bro Neb ddau liw: du
a du.
Mae'r dinasyddion yn ddistaw.
Poblogaeth Bro Neb yw dim.
Prif gynnyrch y wlad yw dim.
Dim, hefyd, ydy'r unig allforiad.
Mae'r farchnad allforio yn brysur.
Ceir glaw trwm, gwyntoedd cryfion
a hefyd ysbeidiau heulog yn dymhorol
ym Mro Neb.
Mae'r haul yn sychu'r pridd du'n llwch
a'r gwynt yn ei chwythu i ffwrdd.
Mae'r glaw yn ei droi'n llaid
a'i olchi i ffwrdd.
Ystyrir y bydd Bro Neb
yn uwchdir o greigiau noeth cyn hir.
Iaith Bro Neb yw Nebeg.
Mewn Nebeg does dim enwau.
Does dim cytseiniaid mewn Nebeg
ond mae dau-ar-bymtheg-ar-hugain
o lafariaid.
Llythyren fwyaf gyffredin Nebeg yw *o*.
Tybir i Nebeg esblygu
neu erydu
o seiniau gwynt, dŵr, hedyddion,
a brefu defaid o bell.
Dau ystyr y gair Nebeg *öowyâo* ydy *ennill*
a *colli*.
Er gwaethaf diffyg pobl nac unrhyw lywodraeth
mae gan Fro Neb wleidyddiaeth fyw.
Mae'r Aflywodraeth yn cyflogi byddin
o ddefaid
sy'n cadw gelynion i ffwrdd.
Prif nodwedd polisi tramor Bro Neb
ydy uchelgais diriogaethol.
Gyda chydweithrediad ei chymdogion
rhagwelir y bydd yn ehangu ei hymerodraeth
yn ddiderfyn.

An outline description of Nihilia

The colours of the national flag of Nihilia are black
and black.
The citizens are mute.
The population of Nihilia is zero.
The country's chief product is nothing.
Nothing is also the leading export
followed by dirt.
The export market thrives.
Nihilia has seasonal snow, heavy rains,
high winds and some sunny spells.
The sun dries the black earth to atoms
and the wind disperses them.
Rain makes of the black earth a slurry
and washes it away.
It is considered that Nihilia will, soon,
be a plate of naked rock.
The language of Nihilia is Nihilish.
In Nihilish there are no nouns.
In Nihilish there are no consonants
but there are thirty-seven vowels.
The most common letter of the alphabet is *o*.
It is believed that Nihilish evolved
or eroded from the sounds of
wind, water, skylarks
and the calls of sheep at a distance.
The two meanings of the Nihilish word *öoôuïâ* are *win*
and *lose*.
Despite the absence
of either people or government
Nihilia has an active politics.
The ungovernment employs a standing army
of sheep
to keep out enemies.
The guiding principle of Nihilish foreign policy
is territorial gain.
It is foreseen that
with the co-operation of its neighbours
the expansion of its empire may be
limitless.

This late

In thirty-three, that year of the giant ape
and the small dictator,
my father watched his younger brother die.

On his own last bed six decades on
he remembered him. Ronald. Twelve.

At that other end of the century
the glass carriage waited
on the unmade road in Walter Street.
Above bared heads, a black plume
nodded on a steaming horse
gesturing how still they were, the grownups,
before the turning of the wheels.

★

Queuing at the lights in rain today I saw
with no tremor of premonition
the same glass carriage
going through on amber
wheel across my path.

Behind the glass was somebody's coffin,
bright-flowered. All else was glossy black
but for some fretted silver round the roof –
the raised whip's spidery arabesque
the ribboned top hat of the coachman angled back,
the trotting pair
all turning out of another man's memory
and into the stream of raindrenched Clios, Subarus,
three cars ahead with a coconut-clacking sound effect.
And yes, there was the black plume nodding forward.

Passers by on pavements, discreetly, rubbernecked.

★

We find meaning where we can,
even in its lack. Once there could be
horror at the end of things made actual
in a feather, painted wood, some glass.

Is it too late now even for the lack to signify,
and must we say, post-Disney, post-war, post so much
that what I saw was more canny than un-,
a cunning funeral-parlour's fashion-trap,
the latest thing to be seen dead in,
jet and retro, death's stretch limo
that can't help but echo Snow White's hearse,
the unmeant promise of happy wakings
purchased with a kiss, a bit of sable bling
put on to turn and not to bare those heads –

or was there some child in the black car following
who'll yet out-innocent all irony,
forget all this and live a life
and then, towards this century's end, aghast
call out some other's name and age
and answer that plume's beckoning at last?

An empty chair, the old man's face

After a photograph by Vesa Lahti

The waxwings whir from rowan trees
   across the margin of the ice.

In the abandoned cottage are
   an empty chair, the old man's face

in monochrome hung on a nail.
   The old are dead, the young are gone

– the waxwings whirred from rowan trees
   across the image of the moon.

The banners of the frozen reeds
   remember how the cold wind tore

the waxwings from the rowan trees
   – or did they really choose to go

from empty chair, from old man's face
   to towers on the farther shore?

Let's gather once in this bright room
and sing the sunset of that home

and sing the chair and sing the face
and sing air whitening under ice

sing the quiet and the roar
and sing the city on the shore.

Birch

I must
cut down
my birch tree.
It clouds my midwindow
hanging its banners
in October riversmoke
is always
the first one
to ruffle
and swivel
flail
in the westerlies
affecting fragility
its skin peeled and shiny
its wood wet and sappy
and not any cop
for making
or burning
– useless for anything
but standing and bending
in its own sleek remakings.
The snappy whippy skyrocket!
Such sprung insistence
such squishy insolence
such delicate success
spell the death of it.
I must rope it
and process it
pull it
out
of
the
sky.

Thaws and disappointments

Come mid-December dawns
the river valley draws on steely chic

the still bare trees composed
like leggy fashion plates in sable tights

veiled in the lace of icy smoke.
Fields that were muddy in Terry-thomas tweeds

turn silverplate, George Clooney sleek
and at the garden table those

eggy-chested jazzing tits
have learned the trick of monochrome

and striking poses for the stills
put on an understated ritz.

Only that idiot toff the sun
reels through the drunken windows

his blazer loud with stripes
all laughing gas, no poise.

His eyeglass burns like lust.
The Garbo east slips off her cool

and blushes orange, turquoise, then hot blue.
Pal Terry skulks back like a caddish fox.

The sky pulls on those criss-cross jet trails like
the diamonds on a pimpish golfer's socks.

We dream of snow

We dream of snow
say, on an endless plateau where
it's falling endlessly through the dark air, or

in some lane we know or think
we know branchsifted to the sunken

way in harmless settling
warm in its emptiness
so *bleak* and *desolate* are lovelinesses now we
dream of snow

the unironic blanket that Joyce spread
over his one green love, no hearse
but a quickening of the dead in weather's
dream – oh, we love we love its down dark feather fall,
affect like Ronald Coleman to recall a

wistful dream of a dream of going back
to some perfected valley, but the fact of
dreaming's in that filmset aeroplane so
decorously crashed in ice and rock –
the stumbling blizzard on some nival plain
is lovelier than the fanfares of arrival

which signify the dream must end.

Definitive annihilation, come
blur us into earth
erase us to completion
whose white hearth is
true home where no one lives
and write
the better rhyme
that restores this page's room with
white

The fiddler's frown

starts somewhere in the earth
a yard beneath his feet
and comes up somehow through
the sprung wood floor
along the channels of his dapper shoes
spreading its sudden branches
like an electric tree
through all of him
bending him leftward tense and tender
     lifting his right elbow so
the elegant ess or eff
of forearm wrist and hand
flexes its delicate muscularity
     tucking his other elbow so
with wrist cocked under
the timber neck he gestures how
he's closed he's open
asking answering
yearning sated
an essential trembling gutsbreadth
from totality or vacuum
or anyway a micron from the nub of
whatever it is
     and really his eyebrows
are the least of it
except that the backwards
brackets on his forehead say
that in this sounding moment
nothing is unimportant
that matter matters
     and the downdrawn brows
like delta-ed effholes vector energy
down his snout
down his folded chin
and out along the woodwork springboard
     into air

Daedalus with a paramotor

A note sang from the fanblade
he strapped onto his back
and from the maze the parachute rose
and yawned and filled its lung
and hit the note of the air

and suddenly he sat
in a piece of sky
and the chair of it carried him
shoulder-high and higher
the filmy glimmer of the not-there disc
shimmering on his back like
that ruffling of nothing
in the little mirage trembling
so rarely on hot roads
himself the plumb-bob of a pendulum
escaped from the clock and beating time
onelegged walking independent
in the sky
the whole thing an Aeolus lyre
over us its
wires singing that

escape is just a tune
is just this flight's small hour
soles slaloming the ether
syncopating with the
leaning shoulders under
that silky skyhook's crescent in its
curve's and swooping's descant to the
dead slow ghost pavane
of the daylight moon

Earth air

This piece of earth's a billowing pavilion
you never quite peg down.
Odd corners have a stone church hammered in –
Patricio, Cwmiou, Cwmdu, Capel y Ffin.
But their grip's uncertain.

   One day the earth will wake and stretch and sigh
and each church will pop its button
                                        and she'll fly.

The near myth

Red kites like gymnasts medal sky
cling to the nothing they almost were

spill wind from twisting tail and wing
and tremble on the beam of air

The wool of the sheep that bit you

Let's knit a mountain
let's knit it from the fleece
that they sheared from the backs
of the mountain-eating race

Let's knit a mountain
the purl and the plain
let's warm it in the sun
and water it with rain

Let's knit it on the place
where the old sheep bit
let's knit it on the ashes
of the fire that we lit

Let's knit it while we work
and knit it while we play
let's knit it from the white fleece
the black and the grey

Let's darn a mountain
let's darn it like a sock
let's darn it where the heel sticks through
a big white rock

Let's darn it in the morning
and darn it in the night
let's darn it from the black fleece
the grey and the white

Let's weave a mountain
let's weave it in the sky
let's weave it where the buzzards
and the red kites fly

Let's chuck the shuttle one way
then chuck it back
let's weave it from the grey fleece
the white and the black

Let's weave it out of horses
and the sweat of our toil
let's weave it from the seeds
that we'll weave into the soil

Let's weave it out of farmyards
let's weave it out of farms
let's weave it of enchantments
let's weave it out of charms

Let's weave it out of armies
let's weave it out of schemes
let's weave out of wooden pegs
let's weave it out of dreams

Let's knit it out of frogspawn
knit it out of air
let's knit a cosy cover
where the world's gone bare

where the sheep go baa
and the cold go *brr*
let's knit it where the larks sing
and nightjars whirr

Let's knit it out of atoms
knit it out of suns
knit it out of layer cake
and soft cream buns

Let's knit it out of rucksacks
knit it out of stars
knit it out of walking boots
and chocolate bars

Let's knit it out of classrooms
knit it out of schools
knit it out of clever kids
knit it out of fools

Let's knit it out of iron
knit it out of lead
we'll knit it for the living
and we'll knit it for the dead

Let's knit it out of fescue
knit it out of ling
let's do a mountain rescue
let's do a highland fling

with a scattering of sheep's wool
a scattering of grain
let's knit it with the heart
and let's knit it with the brain

Let's knit it with the liver
and let's knit it with the lights
let's knit it with a shiver where
the old sheep bites

Let's knit it out of outer space
knit it out of time
knit it with a paintbrush
knit it with a rhyme

that spins along for ever
until the world is old
let's knit it out of silver
let's knit it out of gold

And when we're all too tired
and our knitting days are spent
the world can come and walk upon
a living monument

and larks will nest inside the vest
we knitted years ago
and sheep may go a-munching
where the four winds blow

and the world can come and marvel
or the world can come and scoff –
knit one, purl one,
now cast off.

Acknowledgements

Some poems have appeared in *The Interpreter's House, New Welsh Review, Planet, Poetry Wales* and *Scintilla.*

Versions of several poems first appeared in the pamphlet *Black Mountains* (Mulfran Press), with images by five artists. These, with the original Welsh language versions of some of them (published here for the first time, in parallel text) were responses to the Woollen Line project, organised by artist Pip Woolf, which experimented with repairing fire damage in the Black Mountains in Powys using felts made of low-grade sheep's wool. This gave rise to the Bog-Mawnog exhibition in Brecknock Museum, 2011, initiated by Woolf, of work by five visual artists to which I contributed texts and recorded readings. Bog~Mawnog was funded by the Arts Council of Wales. 'Arrowhead' also arose from this project. Information on The Woollen Line project can be found here: http://woollenline.wordpress.com/

'The churches' was a joint commission by The Royal Ancient Monuments Commission for Wales and *Planet* and was a response to aerial photographs in the Commission's archive.

'The guitar maker Antonio de Torres' draws on a letter translated from the Spanish in Jose L. Romanillos's wonderful book *Antonio de Torres Guitar Maker – His Life and Work* (Element Books, 1987). I've borrowed several phrases from this.

I'm grateful to Dr Lesley Hodgson, who introduced me to the technique that eventually led me to 'Colonus,' and to Cyril Jones for his invaluable advice on the Welsh language material.

I'm grateful to the HALMA Network and Tŷ Cyfieithu Cymru /Translators' House Wales for a scholarship in 2012-13. Several poems in this collection were completed at the Kirjailijatalo, Jyväskylä, Finland in Oct.-Nov. 2012 and as a guest of Goga Publishers at Hostel Situla, Novo Mesto, Slovenia in Jan.-Feb. 2013.

Notes

'What earth thought': researchers have conjectured that most European languages may have evolved from a lost protolanguage spoken in Anatolia in about 9,000 BC. To compare languages and shifts in language they use a fundamental vocabulary of about 200 words called the Dyen List. I've used this list as the rough vocabulary for the poem.

The violinist who gave rise to 'The fiddler's frown' was Colm O'Riain, whom I heard playing in Limerick in 2006.

SEREN

Well chosen words

Seren is an independent publisher with a wide-ranging list which includes poetry, fiction, biography, art, translation, criticism and history. Many of our books and authors have been shortlisted for – or won – major literary prizes, among them the Costa Award, the Man Booker, Forward Prize, and TS Eliot Prize.

At the heart of our list is a good story told well or an idea or history presented interestingly or provocatively. We're international in authorship and readership though our roots are here in Wales (Seren means Star in Welsh), where we prove that writers from a small country with an intricate culture have a worldwide relevance.

Our aim is to publish work of the highest literary and artistic merit that also succeeds commercially in a competitive, fast changing environment. You can help us achieve this goal by reading more of our books – available from all good bookshops and increasingly as e-books. You can also buy them at 20% discount from our website, and get monthly updates about forthcoming titles, readings, launches and other news about Seren and the authors we publish.

www.serenbooks.com